Quinn
at School

Relating, Connecting, and Responding at School

A Book for Children Ages 3-7

Rick H. Warren

AAPC
PUBLISHING

P.O. Box 23173
Shawnee Mission, Kansas 66283-0173
www.aapcpublishing.net

© 2011 AAPC
P.O. Box 23173
Shawnee Mission, Kansas 66283-0173
www.aapcpublishing.net

Publisher's Cataloging-in-Publication

Warren, Rick H.

    Quinn at school : relating, connecting, and responding at school : a book for children ages 3-7 / Rick Warren. -- Shawnee Mission, Kan. : AAPC Pub., c2011.

        p. ; cm.
        ISBN: 978-1-934575-87-1
        LCCN: 2011933607
        Includes bibliographical references.
        Audience: parents, teachers and children ages 3-7.
        Summary: Depicts situations throughout the school day that often cause problems for young children with autism spectrum and related challenges. Ideas for generalization and practice are suggested for use by parents and teachers.

        1. Autistic children--Behavior modification--Juvenile literature. 2. Social skills in children--Study and teaching. 3. Social interaction in children--Study and teaching. 4. Social participation--Study and teaching. 5. Interpersonal relations in children--Study and teaching. 6. (Social skills. 7. Interpersonal relations.) I. Title.

RJ506.A9 W373 2011
618.92/85882--dc23 1108

This book is designed in Avant Garde.
Illustrations: © iClipart.com
Photography: © Photos.com
Printed in the United States of America.

Hope begins in the dark,
the stubborn hope that if you just show up
and try to do the right thing, the dawn will come.

–Anne Lamott

Author's Note

All the tests were done; we sat together in the deserted waiting room, arms draped across the shoulders of the boy who sat, legs dangling, between us. It would be another hour before they called his name to give us the results.

Leaving the clinic, my wife broke into jagged sobs as she clutched our "information packet" to her chest.

"Why's Mommy crying?" the boy asked.

"She's okay. Everything's okay," I lied.

Outside, the warm afternoon air engulfed us in locust song and blossom scent – a perfect summer day. But not for us.

The day your child is "diagnosed" – oh, how I've come to hate that word – is like no other. Some have likened it to the death of a loved one, others to a punch in the gut that leaves you gasping for air. In the days that follow, you try to find your feet: scrambling to arrange therapy and special schooling; rearranging your home in ways that promote language development; reading constantly and beginning the long struggle with insurance companies and school officialdom – anything that will help. After months of grinding work, a program of sorts falls into place. Slow growth and small successes are often the order of the day, and for some families the pace of growth remains glacial. Indeed, over time, parents often come to realize that much of the progress – and many of the breakthroughs – result from their own interventions.

Like so many children, my three-year-old son's central challenge was difficulty initiating or sustaining social contact. In addition to the interventions and resources we already had, what I needed was a highly visual picture book that would help him begin to decode and use the nonverbal cues that make up so much of social communication. What I found was a disappointing lack of high-quality picture books in this area.

I could tell my son wanted to connect, but didn't know how. So we talked; we rehearsed different situations, searching for a step forward. Even so, my son's isolation from his peers only grew when he entered preschool. Each day he seemed more alone, yet each failed interaction only increased my desire to prepare him. I had to do something to help him begin to interact and respond; I had to find a way for him to understand the crucial interactions he kept missing. Soon thereafter, I began writing *Quinn at School*.

During my son's first months of preschool, I tried to capture vignettes that reflected the social challenges (interacting with classmates, greeting teachers, playground politics, art class, library visits, etc.) he faced each school day. Once written, I used *Quinn at School* in print format, but I also began using it in PDF format, letting my son advance the pages on our laptop computer. This digital-book format was highly engaging, and highly effective. Over time, the results I achieved with *Quinn at School* were remarkable: Consistent use of evidence-based practices like social priming, modeling, generalization, and visual support helped my son begin to notice and read nonverbal language; moreover, therapists, teachers, aides, doctors, and special education teachers all noted solid progress in the area of social integration. Finally – and perhaps most important – my son truly enjoyed reading the story and trying out the interactions.

I hope you will find, as I did, that *Quinn at School* is a helpful starting point, a launch pad from which a child can begin to explore and make sense of the intensely social world in which we live.

RHW

Table of Contents

How to Use This Book

On the pages that follow, please find a few suggestions for using *Quinn at School*.

At home...

- Use as a lap book!

- Use in PDF format on your computer! See enclosed CD.

In the classroom ...

- Convert digital content from the PDF version of the book into Mimio Notebook format for use on your Mimio interactive whiteboard system!

- Convert digital content from the PDF version of the book into SMART Notebook format for use on your SMART notebook system!

Extending Learning/Generalization

Quinn at School developed practically, week by week, as I watched my son progress through his first semester of preschool. Its pages contain more than a dozen vignettes, typical scenes from daily kid life. Yet, while the book covers an ample range of situations, it is by no means all-encompassing; indeed, if the lessons taught in the book are to have any lasting value, parents and teachers must make every effort to generalize and extend learning.

To avoid merely providing scripted responses to set situations, *Quinn at School* offers fourteen scenarios that have been specifically chosen for their universality: seeing a friend; greeting a teacher; listening in class; telling how old you are; raising your hand in class; pointing at stuff; asking for help; showing your work; having a snack; sharing stuff; asking kids to play; waiting your turn; answering questions; and saying goodbye. Each scenario provides a foundation upon which further interactions can be formed. What's more, each scenario is ideally accompanied by modeling (i.e., when the kids in the story smile, high-five, or raise their hands, those reading the book should do the same) to raise the level of interaction and, hence, retention. In addition, each scenario is followed by a brief quiz to help with concept formation, such as the following for Seeing a Friend and Asking Kids to Play.

Each scenario is also accompanied by a built-in generalization activity that can be used to explore other avenues for a given social skill. Aside from providing three other scenarios in which a skill (sharing, showing your work, waiting your turn, etc.) may be used, there's a space for kids to individualize the lesson by identifying someone with whom they could practice the skill, such as a teacher, friend, or sibling. Sticking with the Seeing a Friend and Asking scenarios, here are the corresponding practice opportunities.

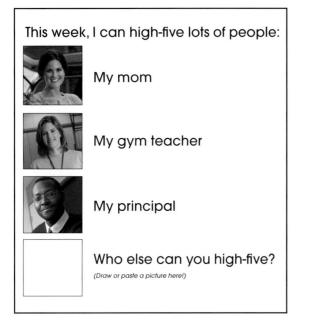 

It's here, in the modeling and generalization sections of each scenario, that interactive classroom technologies such as SMART Board™ and Mimio™ really shine, giving kids the chance to use interactive markers to individualize their work.

Finally, the free poster that comes with the book is a colorful reminder of the important social skills addressed.

My name is Quinn.

I love to smile and run and play and laugh.

But sometimes it's hard
to know what to do …

… or what to say.

When I get to school
in the morning, I see kids I know …

What should I do?

Can you help me decide?

It's FRIENDLY to …

… walk to class together.

It's even FRIENDLIER to ...

... high-five.

And it's SUPER FRIENDLY to …

... high-five and say, "What's up?"

When I see my friends, I should ...

☐ Hide my eyes

☐ High-five

☐ Run and hide

This week, I can high-five lots of people:

 My mom

 My gym teacher

 My principal

 Who else can you high-five?

(Draw or paste a picture here!)

When I get to class, my teacher says, "Good Morning!"

Greeting My Teacher

What should I do?

Can you help me decide?

It's COOL to …

… smile!

It's even COOLER to …

… smile and wave!

And it's SUPER COOL to …

… smile, wave, and say, "Hi!"

When my teacher says, "Good morning!" I should ...

☐ Cross my arms

☐ Scream and yell

☐ Smile, wave, and say, "Hi"

Hi!

This week, I can smile, wave, and say, "Hi!" to lots of people:

 The lunch lady

 The librarian

 The mail carrier

 Who else can you smile, wave, and say, "Hi" to?

(Draw or paste a picture here!)

21

Every morning, the teacher asks us to put away our stuff and sit down.

What should I do?

Can you help me decide?

It's HELPFUL to put away my toy ...

... right away.

It's even more HELPFUL to sit down quietly …

… with my friends.

And it's SUPER HELPFUL to look at the teacher …

… and listen while she teaches.

When my teacher asks me to sit, I should …

☐ Sit quietly and listen

☐ Get a drink of water

☐ Hop on one foot

This week, I can listen to lots of people:

 My dad

 The bus driver

 A policewoman

 Who else can you listen to?

(Draw or paste a picture here!)

In the hall, sometimes a big kid asks ...

... how old I am.

What should I do?

Can you help me decide?

It's GOOD to show …

… with my fingers.

It's even BETTER to count on my fingers …

… by saying, "One, two, three, four, five …"

And it's BEST to count and say, …

When someone asks how old I am, I should …

☐ Draw a picture

☐ Stand on one foot

☐ Count on my fingers and say how old I am

I'm five years old!

This week, I can tell lots of people how old I am:

 My grandpa

 My neighbor

 A firefighter

 Who else can I tell?

(Draw or paste a picture here!)

When the librarian reads us a story ...

What should I do?

Can you help me decide?

It's POLITE ...

... to sit quietly.

It's even more POLITE …

… to watch and sit still while she reads.

And it's SUPER POLITE to raise my hand …

… when I know the answer to a question.

When I know an answer, I should ...

☐ Cover my mouth

☐ Stick out my tongue

☐ Raise my hand

This week, I can raise my hand for lots of things:

 To go to the bathroom

 To get a drink of water

 To show I'm present

 Who else might like it if I raised my hand?

(Draw or paste a picture here!)

Later, the librarian asks which book I want to check out.

Pointing at Stuff

What should I do?

Can you help me decide?

It's O.K. to point ...

... at the book I want.

It's BETTER to point and say …

And it's BEST to point, smile, and say …

That one, please!

When I want something, I should …

☐ Scratch my head

☐ Point, smile and say, "That one, please!"

☐ Tie my shoe

This week, I can point to lots of things:

Foods I like

Friends I see

Planes in the sky

What else can I point to this week?

(Draw or paste a picture here!)

Art is fun, but sometimes …

… I can't find my scissors.

What should I do?

Can you help me decide?

It's NICE to smile and point
to my friend's scissors.

It's even NICER to point and say ...

And it's SUPER NICE to smile, point, and say …

When I see something I need, I should …

☐ Stomp my feet

☐ Hold my nose

☐ Smile, point, and say, "May I borrow that, please?"

This week, I can smile, point, and say "May I borrow that, please?" for lots of things:

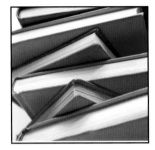 Books I like

 Toys I like

 Colors I like

 What else might you ask to borrow?

(Draw or paste a picture here!)

I'm finished drawing,
and I'm really proud.

What should I do?

Can you help me decide?

It's EXCELLENT to tap my classmate's shoulder …

… and show my work.

It's even more EXCELLENT to raise
my hand and ...

... show my teacher my work.

And it's SUPER EXCELLENT to say …

… and show my work at home.

When I finish painting, I should …

☐ Put my head down

☐ Be very quiet

☐ Tap my friend's shoulder and say, "Check it out!"

This week, I can tap a friend's shoulder and say, "Check it out!" about lots of things:

Pictures I draw

Books I'm reading

People I see

Who might like it if you showed them your work?

(Draw or paste a picture here!)

It's lunch time, and I'm really hungry.

What should I do?

Can you help me decide?

It's OKAY to …

… sit with my friends.

It's even more OKAY...

... to show my friends what I have brought to eat.

And it's SUPER OKAY to …

… talk to my friends about a favorite video game.

When it's lunch time, I should …

☐ Blow bubbles

☐ Show my friends what I have brought and talk about a favorite game

☐ Juggle apples

This week, I can share and talk about lots of things:

 Toys

 Snacks

 My video game

 What else might you talk about and share?

(Draw or paste a picture here!)

Toys are lots of fun …

… but sometimes my friend and I want the same thing.

What should I do?

Can you help me decide?

It's KIND to share …

… with my friend.

It's even KINDER to smile …

… and take turns!

And it's SUPER KIND to smile and say …

Let's play together!

When my friend and I both want the same toy, I should ...

☐ Grab the toy!

☐ Make mean faces

☐ Share a toy and play together!

This week, my friends and I can play together and share lots of stuff:

 The slide

 Toys

 The computer

 Who might you like to play and share with this week?

(Draw or paste a picture here!)

85

At recess, the kids at school …

… play games.

What should I do?

Can you help me decide?

It's FUN to watch …

… and cheer

It's even more FUN to ...

... join in the game!

And it's SUPER FUN to say …

When the kids at school play games, I should …

☐ Wink

☐ Hold up my hand

☐ Ask, "Can I play?"

Can I play?

This week, I can ask, "Can I play?" about lots of things:

 Tag

 Tetherball

 Jump rope

 What other game would you like to play this week?

(Draw or paste a picture here!)

The slide is cool ...

... but sometimes other kids get in the way!

What should I do?

Can you help me decide?

It's PATIENT to wait in line …

… with the other kids.

It's even more PATIENT to smile …

… when the other kids go down .

And it's SUPER PATIENT to say …

When I am waiting my turn, I should ...

☐ Pretend I'm sleeping

☐ Smile and say, "You go first!"

You go first!

☐ Tie my shoes

This week, I can wait my turn for lots of things:

To use the water fountain

To get on the bus

For my turn at sports

What else should you wait for this week?

(Draw or paste a picture here!)

The principal asks if I had fun at recess ...

Answering Questions

What should I do?

Can you help me decide?

It's GREAT to nod "yes!"

It's even GREATER to nod …

… and give a big thumbs-up.

And it's SUPER GREAT to nod,
give a thumbs-up, and say …

When the principal asks if I had fun
at recess, I should ...

☐ Make a funny face

☐ Blow my nose

☐ Give a thumbs-up
and answer

Yeah!
I had fun!

108

This week, I can give a thumbs-up to lots of people:

 The school nurse

 My coach

 The bus driver

 Who else can you give a thumbs-up?

(Draw or paste a picture here!)

It's time to go home, so the teacher says,

What should I do?

Can you help me decide?

It's FRIENDLY to …

… smile!

It's even FRIENDLIER to …

… smile and wave!

And it's SUPER FRIENDLY to …

Goodbye!

… smile, wave, and say, "Goodbye!"

When my teacher says, "Goodbye!" I should ...

☐ Cross my arms

☐ Scream and yell

Goodbye!

☐ Smile, wave, and say, "Goodbye!"

This week, I can wave goodbye to lots of people:

 The janitor

 The secretary

 My friends

 Who else can you wave goodbye to?

(Draw or paste a picture here!)

117

Getting along with people and making friends is super fun when I ...

... smile

... use my hands appropriately

... say a few words

Can I play?

... share

... wait my turn

... and listen.

Bibliography of Selected Resources

Baker, J. (2003). *Social skills training for children and adolescents with Asperger Syndrome and social-communication problems.* Shawnee Mission, KS: AAPC Publishing.

Baker, J. (2001). *The social skills picture book.* Arlington, TX: Future Horizons.

Bareket, R. (2006). *Playing it right!: Social skills activities for parents and teachers of young children with autism spectrum disorders, including Asperger Syndrome and autism.* Shawnee Mission, KS: AAPC Publishing.

Bellini, S. (2006). *Building social relationships: A systematic approach to teaching social interaction skills to children and adolescents with autism spectrum disorders and other social difficulties.* Shawnee Mission, KS: AAPC Publishing.

Buron, K., & Curtis, M. (2004). The *incredible 5-point scale: Assisting students with autism spectrum disorders in understanding social interactions and controlling their emotional responses.* Shawnee Mission, KS: AAPC Publishing.

Buron, K. (2006). *When my worries get too big! A relaxation book for children who live with anxiety.* Shawnee Mission, KS: AAPC Publishing.

Carter, M. A., & Santomauro, J. (2007). *Pirates: An early-years group program for developing social understanding and social competence for children with autism spectrum disorders and related challenges.* Shawnee Mission, KS: AAPC Publishing.

Endow, J. (2009). *Outsmarting explosive behavior: A visual system of supports and intervention for individuals with autism spectrum disorders.* Shawnee Mission, KS: AAPC Publishing.

Gray, C. (2010). *The new Social Story book. 10th anniversary edition.* Arlington, TX: Future Horizons.

Gutstein, S., & Sheely, R. (2002). *Relationship development intervention with young children: social and emotional development activities for Asperger Syndrome, autism, PDD, and NDL.* Philadelphia, PA: Jessica Kingsley Publishers.

Larson, E. M. (2006). *I am utterly unique: Celebrating the strengths of children with Asperger Syndrome and high-functioning autism.* Shawnee Mission, KS: AAPC Publishing.

Larson, E. M. (2007). *Kaleidoscope kid: Focusing on the strengths of children with Asperger Syndrome and high-functioning autism.* Shawnee Mission, KS: AAPC Publishing.

Loomis, J. W. (2008). *Staying in the game: Providing social opportunities for children and adolescents with autism spectrum disorders and other developmental disabilities.* Shawnee Mission, KS: AAPC Publishing.

Manasco, H. (2006). *The way to A: Empowering children with autism spectrum and other neurological disorders to monitor and replace aggression and tantrum behavior.* Shawnee Mission, KS: AAPC Publishing.

Murdock, L., & Khalsa, G. S. (2003). *Joining In! A program for teaching social skills* (video). Shawnee Mission, KS: AAPC Publishing.

Otten, K., & Tuttle, J. (2010). *How to reach and teach children with challenging behavior (K-8): Practical, ready-to-use interventions that work.* San Francisco, CA: Jossey-Bass.

Schneider, C. (2007). *Acting antics: A theatrical approach to teaching social understanding to kids and teens with Asperger syndrome.* Philadelphia, PA: Jessica Kingsley Publishers.

Smith, B., Trautman, M., & Schelvan, R. (2004). *The hidden curriculum: Practical solutions for understanding unstated rules in social situations.* Shawnee Mission, KS: AAPC Publishing.

Snodgrass, C. S. (2008). *What's that look on your face? All about faces and feelings.* Shawnee Mission, KS: AAPC Publishing.

Weiss, M. J. (2008). *Practical solutions for educating young children with high-functioning autism and Asperger Syndrome.* Shawnee Mission, KS: AAPC Publishing.

P.O. Box 23173
Overland Park, Kansas 66283-0173
www.aapcpublishing.net